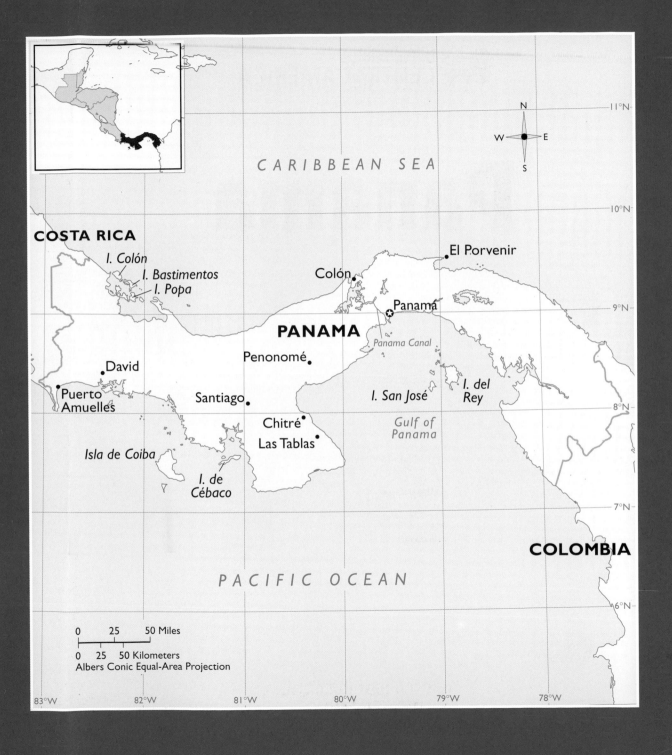

CARIBBEAN SEA

COSTA RICA

N
W E
S

11°N

10°N

I. Colón
I. Bastimentos
I. Popa

Colón

El Porvenir

Panamá

PANAMA

Panama Canal

9°N

David

Penonomé

I. San José

I. del Rey

8°N

Puerto
Amuelles

Santiago

Gulf of
Panama

Isla de Coiba

Chitré
Las Tablas

I. de
Cébaco

7°N

COLOMBIA

PACIFIC OCEAN

6°N

0   25   50 Miles
0   25   50 Kilometers
Albers Conic Equal-Area Projection

83°W   82°W   81°W   80°W   79°W   78°W

DISCOVERING
CENTRAL AMERICA

Panama

DISCOVERING
CENTRAL AMERICA

Panama

Charles J. Shields

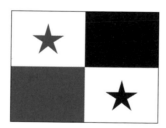

Mason Crest Publishers
Philadelphia

Mason Crest Publishers
370 Reed Road
Broomall PA 19008
www.masoncrest.com

First printing

1 3 5 7 9 8 6 4 2

Library of Congress Cataloging-in-Publication Data
on file at the Library of Congress

ISBN 1-59084-098-4

DISCOVERING
CENTRAL AMERICA

Belize   Guatemala
Central America: Facts and Figures   Honduras
Costa Rica   Nicaragua
El Salvador   Panama

Introduction   6
James D. Henderson

The Isthmus Cut by
        the "Path Between the Seas"   9

Panama's "Geographic Destiny"   15

An Economy Centered on the Canal   23

A Mixed People from All over the World   33

A Rich Cultural Stew   39

Carnaval: The All-Panama Festival   47

Recipes   52

Glossary   54

Project and Report Ideas   56

Chronology   58

Further Reading/Internet Resources   60

For More Information   61

Index   62

Discovering Central America

James D. Henderson

CENTRAL AMERICA is a beautiful part of the world, filled with generous and friendly people. It is also a region steeped in history, one of the first areas of the New World explored by Christopher Columbus. Central America is both close to the United States and strategically important to it. For nearly a century ships of the U.S. and the world have made good use of the Panama Canal. And for longer than that breakfast tables have been graced by the bananas and other tropical fruits that Central America produces in abundance.

Central America is closer to North America and other peoples of the world with each passing day. Globalized trade brings the region's products to world markets as never before. And there is promise that trade agreements will soon unite all nations of the Americas in a great common market. Meanwhile improved road and air links make it easy for visitors to reach Middle America. Central America's tropical flora and fauna are ever more accessible to foreign visitors having an interest in eco-tourism. Other visitors are drawn to the region's dazzling Pacific Ocean beaches, jewel-like scenery, and bustling towns and cities. And everywhere Central America's wonderful and varied peoples are outgoing and welcoming to foreign visitors.

These eight books are intended to provide complete, up-to-date information on the five countries historians call Central America (Guatemala, El Salvador, Honduras, Nicaragua, Costa Rica), as well as on Panama (technically part of South America) and Belize (technically part of North America). Each volume contains chapters on the land, history, economy, people, and cultures of the countries treated. And each country study is written in an engaging style, employing a vocabulary appropriate to young students.

A large ship passes through the "path between the seas"—the Panama Canal.

All volumes contain colorful illustrations, maps, and up-to-date boxed information of a statistical character, and each is accompanied by a chronology, a glossary, a bibliography, selected Internet resources, and an index. Students and teachers alike will welcome the many suggestions for individual and class projects and reports contained in each country study, and they will want to prepare the tasty traditional dishes described in each volume's recipe section.

This eight-book series is a timely and useful addition to the literature on Central America. It is designed not just to inform, but also to engage school-aged readers with this important and fascinating part of the Americas.

Let me introduce this series as author Charles J. Shields begins each volume: *¡Hola!* You are discovering Central America!

A large cargo ship passes through the Panama Canal (opposite). Built in the early 20th century, the canal enabled ships to easily pass from the Atlantic to the Pacific Ocean. (Right) A young native of Panama holds a turtle he has found while snorkeling. Many people come to Panama to enjoy its unspoiled natural resources.

1 The Isthmus Cut by the "Path Between the Seas"

¡HOLA! ARE YOU discovering Panama? Panama offers some of the finest snorkeling, bird watching, and deep-sea fishing in the world. It's a prosperous nation that honors its Amerindian and Spanish past. And don't forget, the Panama Canal. "The Path Between the Seas," as one author titled his history of it, is one of the great engineering marvels of the modern age.

An Arc of Land

The *Isthmus* of Panama is an arc of land joining South and Central America. It stretches 480 miles (772 kilometers) from the South American mainland nation of Colombia on the east to Costa Rica on the west. At its narrowest point, Panama is only 30 miles (50 km) wide, and rarely wider

9

Quick Facts: The Geography of Panama

Location: Middle America, bordering both the Caribbean Sea and the North Pacific Ocean, between Colombia and Costa Rica

Geographic coordinates: 9 00 N, 80 00 W

Area: (slightly smaller than South Carolina)
total: 78,200 sq. km
land: 75,990 sq. km
water: 2,210 sq. km

Borders: Colombia 225 km, Costa Rica 330 km, coastline: 2,850 km

Climate: tropical maritime; hot, humid, cloudy; prolonged rainy season (May to January), short dry season (January to May)

Terrain: interior–mostly steep, rugged mountains and dissected, upland plains; coastal areas–largely plains and rolling hills

Elevation extremes:
lowest point: Pacific Ocean 0 m
highest point: Volcán de Chiriquí 3,475 m

Natural resources: copper, mahogany forests, shrimp, hydropower

Land use:
arable land: 7 percent
permanent crops: 2 percent
permanent pastures: 20 percent
forests and woodland: 44 percent
other: 27 percent
Irrigated land: 320 sq km

than 75 miles (120 km) anywhere else. It has a 720-mile-long (1,160 km) Caribbean coastline, which is rather straight, on its northern shore, and a 1,048-mile-long (1,690 km) Pacific coastline to the south. The Pacific coast is irregular and interrupted by *peninsulas*. A scattering of islands lies offshore on both coasts. The famous canal is 50 miles (80 km) long and cuts the country into eastern and western regions.

The western half of Panama is taken up by a single mountain range, the Serranía de Tabasara. More than 6,500 feet (1,980 m) high near the Costa Rican border, it slopes to less than 1,000 feet (300 m) near the Panama Canal. Several large volcanoes poke above the range. The highest, Barú (formerly known as Chiriquí), reaches 11,400 feet (3,475 m). From the Canal Zone, a long valley runs in a southeasterly direction, separated from the Caribbean by the narrow mountain ranges of the Cordillera de San Blas and Serranía del Darien. On the opposite side, two ranges separate the valley from the Pacific—the Serranías de Maje and del Sapo, and the Sierra de Jungurudo.

There are hundreds of islands near the Panamanian coasts. The two major *archipelagos* are the San Blas and Bocas del Toro chains in the Caribbean Sea, although the best snorkeling, diving, and deep-sea fishing are to be found in the Pacific near Coiba Island and the Pearl Islands.

The Distance-Saving Canal

The Panama Canal extends approximately 50 miles from Panama City on the Pacific Ocean to Colón on the Caribbean Sea. It is widely considered to be one of the world's greatest engineering achievements. The United States is the largest user of the Canal in terms of cargo *tonnage*, although

Panama is located within the tropics, and has many rainforests. This small rainforest waterfall is located in Soberania Park.

Asian countries are beginning to close the gap. About 12 percent of U.S. seaborne international trade, in terms of tonnage, passes through the Canal annually. Ships bound for Japan from the east coast of the United States save about 3,000 miles by going through the Canal. Ships sailing from Ecuador to Europe save about 5,000 miles.

The Canal Zone lies in rainforest, which covers the northwestern portion of the country and much of the eastern half. The western half of Panama, remember, is high and mountainous. Although Panama's neighbor, Costa Rica, is well known for the variety of its wildlife, Panama actually has a greater number of *flora* and *fauna* species and more land set aside for preservation. Panamanians like to remark that in Costa Rica, 20 tourists try to see one beautiful quetzal bird, but in Panama, one person can see 20 of them at once.

A Macaw sits patiently in a tree on Isla Grande, Panama. Like many other countries of Central America, Panama has a wide variety of bird and animal species, as well as many beautiful plants and trees.

Tropical Weather

Located well within the tropics, Panama is refreshed by easterly *trade winds*. Tropical climates run throughout the country, except at higher elevations west of the Canal Zone. Winters tend to be drier than summers.

Rain varies, depending on location. Along the Pacific coastal plain and in the eastern interior valley, annual precipitation ranges between 55 and 126 inches (140 and 320 centimeters). There may be three to five months without rain. Lighter rainfall along the Pacific gives rise to more grasslands and scrubby, seasonally leafless forest cover.

Along the northern Caribbean shoreline and in the mountains, annual rainfall almost always exceeds 126 inches (320 centimeters) and may reach as much as 236 inches (600 centimeters). Rainless periods are uncommon and rarely last more than one or two months. Heavier rainfall along the Caribbean shoreline provides for a tropical rainforest.

In general, Panama has two seasons. The dry season lasts from January to mid-April, and the rainy season from mid-April to December. Rainfall is heavier on the Caribbean side of the highlands, though most people live on or near the Pacific coast. Temperatures are typically hot in the lowlands—between 70 and 90° F (21 to 32° C)—and cool in the mountains—between 50 and 64° F (10 and 18° C). These vary little throughout the year.

Mireya Moscoso (opposite) greets some 25,000 supporters after being sworn in as president of Panama on September 1, 1999, in Panama City's National Stadium. Her son Ricardo is on the left. (Right) U.S. Marines patrol the Canal Zone in 1989 during Operation Just Cause. This military action was intended to protect the canal and capture Panamanian ruler Manuel Noriega.

2 Panama's "Geographic Destiny"

PANAMA'S HISTORY has been shaped by the ambitions of great powers. From the first arrival of the Spanish until now, Panama's modern history and identity have been tied to its "geographic destiny." In other words, how its fortunes rose and fell on the world stage has always reflected how important the Isthmus was to other nations. For nearly 400 years, the dream of a trans-isthmian canal, and then the building of it, focused the world's attention on Panama, the tiny land bridge joining North and South America

The Royal Road

Rodrigo de Bastidas, sailing westward from Venezuela in 1501 in search of gold, was the first European to explore the Isthmus of Panama. A

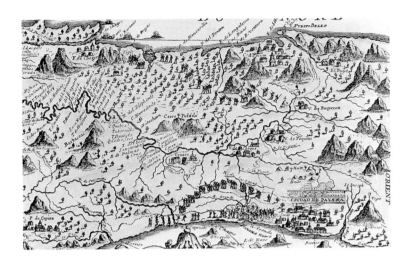

A 16th-century woodcut map of Panama. The region was a Spanish possession in the New World until the countries of Central America broke away from Spain in 1821.

year later, Christopher Columbus visited the Isthmus and established a short-lived settlement. In 1513, Vasco Núñez de Balboa undertook a long march from the Atlantic to the Pacific, proving that the Isthmus was indeed the path between the seas.

As a result, Panama quickly became the crossroads and marketplace of Spain's empire in the New World. The overland route across the Isthmus became known as the *Camino Real*, or Royal Road.

To lay down the Royal Road, the **conquistadors** started out from Santa María la Antigua del Darien in Panama, the first mainland settlement in the Americas, founded in 1510. Armed men headed south and west to build settlements along the road for defense. Two outposts had been completed, and the Spanish were pushing toward the Pacific coast, when Amerindians attacked. A rescue party, under the command of Captain Antonio Tello de Guzman, beat back the assault. Work on the road continued, snaking southward, through rainforest and across the Isthmus. At a tiny Amerindian fishing village, the road builders reached the western coast, joining the Atlantic and Pacific Oceans.

Panama remained part of the Spanish empire for 300 years, until 1821. Spanish ships carrying cargos of gold and silver from South America unloaded them on Panama's Pacific side. The treasures were then hauled by wagons across the Isthmus, and loaded again aboard ships bound for Spain. The Spanish had hopes for a canal through Panama, but instead remained content with the Royal Road for centuries.

Building the Canal

From 1880 to 1900, a French company led by Ferdinand de Lesseps attempted unsuccessfully to construct a sea-level canal on the site of the present Panama Canal. In November 1903, with U.S. and French support, Panama proclaimed its independence from Colombia and concluded the Hay/Bunau-Varilla Treaty with the United States.

The treaty granted rights to the United States to act freely in a zone roughly 10 miles wide and 50 miles long. In that zone, the U.S. would build a canal, then administer, fortify, and defend it for all time, according to the treaty. In 1914, the United States completed the existing 50-mile (83 km) *lock* canal, one of the world's greatest engineering triumphs. Beginning in the 1960s, however, a *nationalist* movement inside Panama called for renegotiating the treaty with the United States.

The Military Takes Over

From 1903 until 1968, Panama was a democracy. It was steered, though, by a commercially minded *elite*. The canal was "the goose that laid the golden egg" to those who earned an income from it, and they protected their interests by controlling the government.

Then, beginning in the 1950s, the Panamanian military upset the balance of power. In October 1968, president Dr. Arnulfo Arias Madrid was ousted by the National Guard after only 10 days in office. The commander of the National Guard, Brigadier General Omar Torrijos, established a military *junta* government. Torrijos' regime was harsh and corrupt, but his policies benefiting Panama's poor won him widespread support. In his dealings with foreign powers, he made Panama a headstrong and difficult partner.

Torrijos' death in 1981 heightened the power of the Panama Defense Force (PDF), a combination of military and civilian leaders that sought to continue military rule. In 1984, the PDF won most of the seats in the Legislative Assembly, despite charges of corruption. At the head of the PDF was General Manuel Noriega.

The rivalry between wealthy civilian groups and the Panamanian military reached a crisis in the summer of 1987. In reaction to a government clampdown on media and *civil liberties*, more than 100 business, *civic*, and religious groups organized antigovernment demonstrations. The United States *froze* economic and military assistance to Panama because of an attack on the U.S. embassy. The government of Panama countered in December 1987 by expelling the U.S. Agency for International Development from the country. Tensions between the two nations increased further when General Noriega was *indicted* in U.S. courts in February 1988 on drug trafficking charges. In April, U.S. president Ronald Reagan froze Panamanian government assets in U.S. banks and prohibited payments by American agencies, firms, and individuals to the Noriega *regime*.

When national elections were held in May 1989, Panamanians voted for the anti-Noriega candidates by a margin of over three to one. However, the Noriega regime promptly declared the election invalid.

By the fall of 1989, the regime was barely clinging to power. An unsuccessful attempt in October at overthrowing Noriega produced a bloody defense by his Dignity Battalions, which consisted of hand picked, loyal soldiers. Their purpose was to terrorize the general's enemies.

On December 20, 1989, President George Bush ordered the U.S. military into Panama to protect U.S. lives and property, to defend the Canal, and to capture Noriega. Operation Just Cause lasted only seven days, at the end of which Noriega surrendered. He is now serving a 40-year sentence in Florida for drug trafficking.

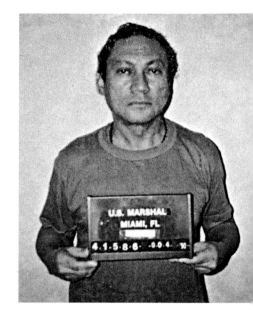

This photograph of Manuel Antonio Noriega was taken after his arrest and trial on drug trafficking charges. Noriega is currently serving a long jail sentence in the United States.

Rebuilding Democracy

Panamanians moved quickly to rebuild their civilian government. On December 27, 1989, Panama's Electoral Tribunal certified the May 1989 election results that Noriega had earlier thrown out and confirmed the victory of President Guillermo Endara.

Five years later, in 1994, Ernesto Pérez Balladares won the presidency

U.S. president George Bush meets with Ernesto Balladares in Panama during 1990.

in an election monitored by an international team of observers. The campaign was Panama's largest, with seven candidates for the presidency, over 2,500 for the legislature, 2,000 for mayoral posts, and more than 10,000 at the local level.

On May 2, 1999, Mireya Moscoso, widow of a popular politician, defeated candidate Martín Torrijos, son of the late dictator. The elections were judged free and fair. Moscoso took office on September 1, 1999.

The Bumpy History of Canal Negotiations

Under the 1903 Hay/Bunau-Varilla Treaty, the United States acquired rights to build and operate a canal in Panama for all time. It also acquired the Canal Zone—a 553-square-mile area in which the United States exercised the rights, power, and authority of an independent state. However, in January 1964, anti-United States riots over control of the canal resulted in the deaths of four U.S. Marines and more than 20 Panamanians.

In an effort to reopen the terms of the 1903 treaty, United States and Panamanian negotiators met in June 1967. New treaties about the existing canal, a possible second canal, and defense issues came out of the talks, but neither country ratified these treaties. In 1970, the Torrijos government publicly rejected them.

In 1973, Secretary of State Henry Kissinger and his Panamanian counterpart, Juan Antonio Tack, successfully laid down a set of principles to guide the creation of new treaties. On September 7, 1977, U.S. president Jimmy Carter and General Omar Torrijos signed the Panama Canal Treaties at the headquarters of the Organization of American States (OAS) in Washington, D.C. The Panamanian people approved the new treaties in a *plebiscite* held on October 23, 1977. The U.S. Senate ratified the Panama Canal Treaty on April 18, 1978. It also ratified the Neutrality Treaty on March 16, 1978, guaranteeing that the canal would be open to all nations. The treaties went into effect October 1, 1979.

Under the new treaties, the United States was responsible for operating and defending the canal until December 31, 1999. Since that date, the United States and Panama have together maintained the canal's neutrality. Merchant and naval vessels of all nations have access to the canal and pay tolls. However, it remains the United States' responsibility to ensure that the canal remains open and secure. When the new treaties were ratified in the U.S. Congress, a condition added by the Senate allowed the United States and Panama to negotiate a new treaty after 1999, if both countries agreed.

Day-to-day responsibility for managing the canal has passed into the hands of Panama. There is no longer any U.S. military base near the Panama Canal. Panama receives an annual share of toll *revenue* from each ship passing through the canal, a portion of which is used to maintain the path between the seas.

(Opposite) A Panamanian worker harvests greens near Guadalupe. (Right) A worker loads a stem of bananas into a truck at the El Lidice farm in Puerto Armuelles. Farming is actually a small part of Panama's economy—most of the country's economic activity is centered around the Panama Canal and the Colón free trade zone

3 An Economy Centered on the Canal

PANAMA'S ECONOMY is primarily based on providing services having to do with the Panama Canal and the Colón Free Zone— the world's second-largest *free trade zone* after Hong Kong. Colón is a city in north-central Panama. The Colón Free Zone is a wholesale distribution center where goods of any kind—including raw materials, like wood or minerals, and machinery—may be imported, stored, modified, distributed, processed, assembled, repacked, and then re-exported without paying *custom duties*—taxes on exports and imports.

Since receiving control of the canal in 1999, Panama has been trying to depend less on its old economic ties with the United States. However, the U.S. remains the largest market for Panama's goods.

23

A Services Hub of the World

Since the Spanish conquest of the New World, the Isthmus of Panama has served as a primary route of transportation and commerce between the Pacific and Atlantic oceans. As the second chapter pointed out, Panama quickly became the crossroads and marketplace of Spain's empire in the New World.

Then, during the mid-19th century, the first railroad to connect the opposite shores of the Americas was built across the Isthmus, largely for prospectors going to the goldfields of California. Panama's economy, then as now, rested solidly on being a transportation hub in the Western Hemisphere. After French attempts to build a canal across the Isthmus failed, the United States completed the project in 1914.

Today, transportation and commerce in Panama continues to center on the region surrounding the canal. A railroad and trans-isthmian highway connect the two shores of Panama. A petroleum pipeline across western Panama opened in 1982. The Omar Torrijos International Airport in Panama City serves as a major airline intersection for all of Central and South America.

Building the canal created many services related to shipping, which still pour hundreds of millions of dollars annually into the Panamanian economy. Among these are warehousing, insurance, banking, registering ships, and maintaining the canal itself.

Panama earns revenue from fees charged to every ship that passes through the canal, too. Every year, more than 13,000 deep-water ships, under the flags of some 79 nations, move through Miraflores to Gatun locks. The system of locks enables ships weighing thousands of tons to navigate the canal's 85-foot change in elevation. By traveling through the canal, rather than south around Cape Horn at the tip of South America, shipping companies save tens of thousands of dollars. Many nations and investors have found it convenient to locate their financial operations near the canal as well.

The government of Panama works to promote its reputation as an international trading, banking, and services center. In early 1998, Panama enacted a new banking law intended to detect and deter *money laundering*, an abuse that became widespread under the dictatorships of Torrijos and Noriega.

Panama continues to fight against illegal narcotics, another problem left over from the Noriega years. The country's nearness to major cocaine-

Panamanian police destroy illegal drugs captured between July and September 2000—2,300 pounds (1,050 kg) of cocaine, 1,700 pounds (760 kg) of marijuana, and 30 pounds (13.5 kg) of heroin. Central America is a key region in the drug trade, as experts estimate that 60 percent of cocaine passes through Central America. Panama has worked hard to stop drug traffickers.

producing nations and its role as a commercial and financial crossroads, make it a key player in the drug war. Panama works closely with the U.S. Treasury Department's Financial Crimes Enforcement Network in keeping drug lords from stashing their money in Panama.

One of the major challenges facing the Panamanian government today is how to put to good use the land and buildings that formerly belonged to the United States. When the United States turned over control of the canal to Panama in 1999, it also **ceded** 70,000 acres of U.S. military land and more than 5,000 buildings. Panama suddenly came into a great deal of developed real estate. However, it must also find a way to replace jobs and income lost when the U.S. military stopped administering and guarding the canal. Estimates of how much the U.S. Department of Defense contributed to the Panamanian economy range from $170 million to $350 million annually.

The Colón Free Zone

Located on the Atlantic side of the canal, the Colón Free Zone was created in 1948. In just over half a century, it has become the largest free zone in the Western Hemisphere and is now second in the world only to Hong Kong.

Wholesalers and retailers travel to the Free Zone because they can buy consumer products either by the container load or in smaller quantities. Zone importers specialize in bringing in container loads of goods, and breaking them down into smaller shipments for resale. In a sense, the zone is a giant discount warehouse with no taxes added to sales.

A total of 1,780 domestic and international companies are now based in

Quick Facts: The Economy of Panama

Per capita income (2001): $7,600

Natural resources: Hydroelectric power, forest products, fisheries products.

Industry (25 percent of GDP*): food and drink processing, paper and paper products, metalworking, petroleum products, chemicals, printing, mining, refined sugar, clothing, furniture, construction

Agriculture (8 percent of GDP): bananas, rice, corn, coffee, sugarcane, vegetables, livestock, shrimp.

Services (67 percent of GDP): Finance, insurance, canal-related services, Colón Free Zone.

Foreign trade (1998): Exports $640 million: bananas, 33 percent; shrimp, 11 percent; sugar, 4 percent; coffee, 2 percent; clothing, 5 percent; other, 45 percent.

Unemployment rate: 13.1 percent.

Economic growth rate: 3.1 percent

Currency exchange rate (2002): 1 balboa = U.S. $1.

* GDP or gross domestic product—the total value of goods and services produced in a year

the Free Zone, creating more than 14,000 jobs. In 2001, these companies imported a huge range of commodities, valued at more than $5.2 billion, while re-exports from the Zone amounted to $5.9 billion.

While the Far East is by far the biggest single source of supplies to the Free Zone, 70 percent of its re-exports are to South America, followed by Central America and the Caribbean. Electronics and clothing are the main exports, followed by a range of products, including watches, cosmetics, shoes, textiles, and pharmaceuticals.

The "Non-Canal" Economy

The rest of Panama's economy—the approximately 30 percent that

Fishing boats are tied to the a dock near the public market in Panama City. Fishing is an important part of Panama's economy. The annual value of its catch is greater than the total fishing income of the other Central American countries combined.

doesn't have to do with the canal—is based on activities that are typical of most Central American countries.

Agriculture is a way of life for nearly a third of the Panamanians. Most are impoverished and provide food for themselves on small farms. Small-scale farming provides grain crops, vegetables, and fruits. In Panama, unlike most Central American nations, rice is traditionally more common in dishes than corn.

From plantations and large estates come an array of agricultural goods for export. From Panama's westernmost lowlands come bananas and cacao, and from the highlands, coffee. Sugar production and cattle ranching tend to be concentrated along the Pacific coast west of the Canal Zone.

Fishing is an important component of the Panamanian economy. The value of Panama's catch of fish is more than all of its Central American neighbors combined. Nearly a fifth of Panama's foreign income is earned from the sale of shrimp and fishmeal.

Although nearly one in three people work in agriculture, it contributes less than one-third to Panama's economy. Manufacturing, on the other hand, generates about one-fourth of the country's total gross domestic product (GDP)—the value of goods and services produced in a year. This difference shows that a large, low-skill section of the population is engaged in low-income farming, an imbalance that most poor countries face.

Manufacturing in Panama is devoted to food processing, textiles, clothing, paper, and furniture. The distance of Panama from core markets like Mexico City and Managua, Nicaragua, slows its sale of manufactured products to neighboring countries. Quicker and cheaper transportation is needed. A refinery located near the canal processes petroleum imported from Venezuela, Ecuador, and Mexico, which is then sold to ships passing through the Canal. The refinery also makes aviation fuel for aircraft.

The U.S./Panama Relationship

After the return of democracy to Panama in the late 1980s, Panama's economy steadily improved. Still, Panama struggles to overcome an important challenge: freeing itself from dependence on the United States.

Trade with the United States makes up a lopsided 40 percent of Panama's total merchandise trade, even though the country is surrounded by potential trading partners. In 1998, for instance, U.S. merchandise exports to Panama were $1.3 billion; U.S. imports from Panama were $280 million, for an overall U.S. trade surplus of just over $1 billion. This means that Panama purchased far more from the United States than it sold, drying up loan money available for investment in Panama.

Also, U.S. companies play a large role in the Panamanian economy. Some 100 U.S. companies operate in Panama. They are particularly active in banking, bananas, ports, and other services. These companies create local jobs, but most of their profit goes back to the United States instead of staying in Panama.

On a positive note, the hope of greater economic independence for Panama is held out by the Panama Canal Treaties. By transferring the Canal and U.S. military properties to local control, Panama received a giant income-generating piece of technology.

Did You Know?

- Panama's government is a constitutional democracy.
- The capital is Panama City.
- Panama became independent from Spain on November 28, 1821. At the time it was part of the South American country of Colombia. It became independent from Colombia on November 3, 1903.

Moreover, Panama no longer bears the cost of maintaining a military: Protection of the Canal is guaranteed by the United States. In addition, spending by the United States on civic and business projects pumps several million dollars annually into the Panamanian economy.

Cultural ties between the two countries remain strong, and many Panamanians come to the United States for higher education and advanced training. About 6,000 Americans live in Panama, most of whom are retirees from the Panama Canal Commission and individuals who hold *dual nationality*. The number of U.S. tourists to Panama averages around 4,000 a year.

(Opposite) Colorful *molas*, made from square pieces of fabric, are part of the traditional costume for women. Made by the Kuna Indians to be sewed onto shirts or blouses, *molas* are decorated in many ways, such as with animals or geometric patterns. (Right) A rancher sits atop his mount on a dirt track in Chiriqui.

4 A Mixed People from All Over the World

THE CULTURE, CUSTOMS, and language of the Panamanians are mainly Caribbean Spanish. Most of the population is *mestizo* (mixed Spanish and Indian), or mixed Spanish, Indian, Chinese, and West Indian. Spanish is the official language, although many Panamanians in business and the professions speak English, too. More than half the population lives in or near Panama City. Not many people live in the countryside.

The Most Racially Diverse

Panama's importance as a crossroads between two oceans brought together people from all over the world. Except for Belize, the population in Panama is racially more diverse than elsewhere in Central America.

Quick Facts: The People of Panama

Population: 2,808,268

Ethnic groups: 70 percent *mestizo* (mixed Amerindian and white); 14 percent mixed Amerindian, Asian, and African; 10 percent white; 6 percent Amerindian.

Age structure:
0–14 years: 31 percent
15–64 years: 63 percent
65 years and over: 6 percent

Population growth rate: 1.34 percent

Birth rate: 19.53 births/1,000 population

Death rate: 4.95 deaths/1,000 population

Infant mortality rate: 20.8 deaths/1,000 live births

Life expectancy at birth:
total population: 75.47 years
male: 72.74 years
female: 78.31 years

Total fertility rate: 2.32 children born per woman

Religions: 85 percent Roman Catholic; 15 percent Protestant.

Languages: Spanish (official); English, 14 percent (many Panamanians are bilingual)

Literacy: 90.8 percent (1995 est.)

*All figures 2001 estimates, unless otherwise noted.

In the early 16th century when Spanish explorers arrived, more than 60 Indian tribes lived in Panama. They were related to the Mayas of Guatemala and Mexico and the Chibchas of Colombia. The Spanish scattered them, however, bringing slaves from Africa to build their settlements. Later, merchants arrived to do business with the traffic between two oceans. Asians offered sugarcane, mangos, rice, and silk for sale. Europeans and North Americans cleared rainforest land for plantations that grew potatoes, tomatoes, bananas, and pineapples.

The gold rush in California in the mid-19th century ignited a new wave of worldwide commerce. As thousands of prospectors arrived on their way to the goldfields of California, a U.S. company hired Caribbean blacks, Irish, and Chinese to lay track for the first trans-isthmian railroad, adding still more new faces to Panama's population. The French arrived at the turn of the century, with great conviction, to construct the canal, bringing with them a new wave of Italian, Hindu, and Caribbean workers.

A Blending That Continues

Today 70 percent of Panamanians are *mestizo*; 14 percent are mixed Amerindian, Asian, and African; 10 percent are white; and 6 percent are Amerindian. Many people have ancestors who were African slaves. The *mestizo* and mixed populations are concentrated within the Canal Zone and along the Pacific lowlands of western Panama. A majority of Panamanians are Roman Catholics. Spanish is the official language, although English and Indian dialects are also spoken. The Amerindians are located in isolated highland pockets and along the Caribbean shoreline east of the Canal Zone. There are three major Indian groups: the Kunas on the San Blas Islands off the Caribbean coast, the Emberá in the province of Darien, and the Guaymies in Chiriquí, Bocas del Toro, and Veraguas provinces.

A Panamanian woman wears *trembleques*—hair ornaments made of beads and wire that shake, or tremble, when she dances.

Native Americans, like the Kuna Indians, make up about 6 percent of Panama's population. This Kuna woman, seated on a brightly decorated table at a festival, has decorated her legs for the occasion.

This blending of peoples and cultures created a rich Panamanian way of life. At festivals in Panama City, African drums can be heard accompanying European songs and guitar playing. Along the Caribbean coast, the descendants of slaves present dances, costumes, and music that pay tribute to the past. In Portobelo, the main port of the Caribbean, annual fairs have parade floats that are both Spanish and European. Panamanians like to say their hospitality comes from interacting with so many different kinds of people in history.

In recent years, the Colón Free Zone and the Banking District in Panama City have attracted large numbers of foreigners who are living in Panama to conduct business. Conversations can be heard in Arabic, Hebrew, English, Chinese, Hindi, and Japanese as businesspeople do business beside the all-important Canal.

Half Live Near the Canal

Panama has one of the slowest population growth rates in Central America.

The population of Panama is about 2.8 million, of whom about half are clustered near the Canal Zone. Most of the remainder live in the Pacific lowlands west of the Canal Zone. Other parts of the country are sparsely populated. Two of the largest cities—Panama City, the capital, with a population of nearly 700,000, and Colón with almost 70,000 inhabitants—lie at the Pacific and Atlantic entrances to the Panama Canal.

The education system of Panama is separated into three levels: primary school (six years), secondary school (six years), and university or higher education. The first six years of primary education are required for all children. A high percentage goes on to enroll in secondary school. More than 65,000 Panamanian students attend the University of Panama, the Technological University, and the University of Santa María La Antigua, a private Catholic institution. Including smaller colleges, there are 14 institutions of higher education in Panama.

Panama has one of the highest literacy rates in Central America. More than 90 percent of Panamanians over 15 years of age can read and write.

(Opposite) A cobblestone street leads up to this large building, which dates back to Panama's colonial period. (Right) The skyline of Panama City, the largest city in Panama. Located near the site of the original Spanish settlement in the region, Panama City today has a population of about 700,000.

5 A Rich Cultural Stew

PANAMA'S CULTURE REFLECTS its unique ethnic mix. Indian tribes, West Indian groups, *mestizos*, Chinese, Middle Eastern, and North American immigrants have all contributed ingredients to this cultural stew, creating a rich tradition.

Brightly colored national dress is worn during local festivals and Carnaval season, especially for traditional folk dances like the *tanborito*. Lively salsa—a mixture of Latin American popular music, rhythm and blues, jazz, and rock—is a Panamanian specialty. Indian influences stand out in handicrafts, such as the famous Kuna Indian *molas*—colored fabrics stitched with geometric and animal designs. Traditional arts in Panama include woodcarving, weaving, dressmaking, ceramics, and mask making.

39

Modern skyscrapers of glass and steel rise behind the solid Baroque-style facade of this church. Nearly all Panamanians are Christian.

The National Costume

Panama's folklore is fully expressed in its traditional dances, its colorful *pollera*—the national costume—and *tembleques* (hair ornaments) worn by women. Embroidered, long-sleeved shirts, calf-high trousers, and a straw *Montuno* hat is the national costume worn by men.

The *pollera* begins with a petticoat, or petticoats, of row after row of finely tucked muslin. Over this goes a full, ankle-length skirt of wide bands, separated by lace whose pattern is the same as that embroidered or appliquéd on the white lawn, or linen, of the *pollera*. It is not unusual for several women to work for months to complete the petticoats and skirt.

The blouse has a deep, embroidered or appliquéd band, edged in lace and gathered onto a neckband, through which is woven yarn ending, front and back, in big pompoms. The color of the yarn must be the same as the color of the ribbons, which are fastened to the front and back of the skirt. Flat velvet slippers are always worn with the *pollera*.

Into the wearer's hair go gold-edged combs and anywhere from a dozen to four dozen pairs of *tembleques*—hair ornaments made of beads or tinsel fastened onto hairpins or wire. Their name comes from the fact that they tremble when their wearer dances.

Countryside *polleras* differ from their big-city cousins in that they have no embroidery or appliqué. Also, they are made from bright-colored calico or some other cotton goods. Native straw hats are always worn to complete the outfit.

Panama City and Colón

The capital of Panama is a modern, thriving commercial center stretching six miles (10 km) along the Pacific coast from the ruins of Panamá Viejo in the east to the edge of the Panama Canal in the west.

The old district of San Felipe (also known as Casco Antiguo or Casco Viejo) juts into the sea on the southwestern side of town. It's an area of decaying colonial grandeur, striking architecture, peeling paint, and romantic balconies. Attractions include the 17th-century Metropolitan Church, the Interoceanic Canal Museum of Panama, the Plaza de Bolívar, the presidential palace, the History Museum of Panama, and the sea wall built by the Spaniards four centuries ago. The Banking District, centered on the Via España, Panama's main street, is the complete opposite, with gleaming new buildings and "big city" entertainment. Attractions on the edges of Panama City include the Panama Canal, the 16th-century ruins of Panamá Viejo, the Summit Botanical Gardens and Zoo, the tropical rainforest of the Parque Nacional Sobreranía, and the 655-acre (265-hectare) Parque Nacional Metropolitana.

Panama City is **duty**-free, and luxury goods from all over the world can be purchased at a saving of at least one-third. Local items include leather-wear, patterned and beaded necklaces made by Guaymí Indians, *molas* sewn by the Kuna Indians, native costumes, handicrafts of carved wood, ceramics, papier mâché artifacts, macramé, and mahogany bowls. International bargains include English china, Irish linen, Japanese electronics, and Swiss watches, all in the windows of shops on the Via España.

A Kuna Indian woman sews a *mola* in a Panama City marketplace. In addition to local crafts, goods from all over the world are available in the shops of Panama's largest city.

Food and Drink

Because Panama is an international crossroads, a variety of cuisines are available. French, Spanish, and American food is available in all restaurants and hotels in Panama City and Colón. There is a huge selection of excellent restaurants in Panama City, as well as other main cities. There are also several Oriental restaurants.

A mixture of fried meat, peppers, and cornmeal dough is placed inside a cornhusk to make a *tamale*—a popular Panamanian dish.

Native cooking on the other hand reminds North Americans of Creole cuisine—hot and spicy. Dishes include *ceviche* (fish marinated in lime juice, onions, and peppers), *patacones de plátano* (fried plantain), *sancocho* (Panamanian stew with chicken, meat, and vegetables), *tamales* (seasoned pie wrapped in banana leaves or corn husks), and *carimañolas* and *empanadas* (turnovers filled with meat, chicken, or cheese).

The Island Cultures

The islands of the San Blas Archipelago, 30 minutes by air from Panama City, are strung out along the Caribbean coast of Panama from the Golfo de San Blas nearly all the way to the Colombian border. They are home to the Kuna Indians, who administer the 378 islands independently with little input from the Panamanian government. The Kuna Indians maintain their own economic system, language, customs, and culture, with distinctive dress, legends, music, and dance.

Kuna women make rainbow-colored fabrics called *molas*, stitched with fish, birds, jungle animals, and geometric designs. The Kuna men still fish from canoes as they did before Columbus came. They also still climb coconut trees for something fresh and cool to drink each morning, just as they have for untold centuries.

The economy of the islands is based on coconut sales, fishing, and tourism. Visitors come for the good diving, snorkeling, and swimming. The best diving conditions are between April and June. The coral reefs here are among the oldest in the world and are studied by marine biologists.

On the Pacific side, Contadora, one of the Pearl Islands, features unspoiled beaches, spectacular sailfish, and water sports everywhere—snorkeling, scuba, windsurfing, jet-skiing, and sailing. There is tennis and golf, too.

Did You Know?

- Panama's current constitution was adopted on October 11, 1972. Major reforms were made in 1983 and in 1994.
- The voting age is 18.
- Panama's government consists of an executive branch, a legislative branch, and a judicial branch.
- The president and vice president are elected on the same ticket by popular vote for five-year terms.
- There are 72 seats in the Asamblea Legislativa (Legislative Assembly). Members are elected by popular vote to serve five-year terms.
- Panama's legal system is based on a system of civil laws. Nine judges are appointed for 10-year terms on the Corte Suprema de Justicia (Supreme Court of Justice).
- Political parties in Panama include Arnulfista Party, or PA; Christian Democratic Party, or PDC; Civic Renewal Party, or PRC.

Then there is Taboga, also in the Pacific—the Island of Flowers. There's never a traffic jam on this island because there are no cars. Only bikes are used for transportation. Tropical flowers grow wild here in dazzling splashes of color, and 100,000 pelicans nest on the rocky beaches, almost within waving distance of Panama City and the Canal. Taboga's tiny church lays claim to being the second oldest in the Western Hemisphere.

Did You Know?

- Panama's flag is divided into four equal rectangles. The top quadrants are white (hoist side) with a blue five-pointed star in the center and plain red. The bottom quadrants are plain blue (hoist side) and white with a red five-pointed star in the center.
- The national bird of Panama is the harpy eagle.
- The national flower of Panama is *Espíritu Santo,* a species of orchid.

Because of Panama's tropical climate, locals and tourists alike enjoy golf, tennis, and water sports most days of the year. Baseball is also enjoyed and is not just a national pastime, it's a national passion.

(Opposite) The queen of Panama's Carnaval, Maite Bilboa, dances to music during a parade in Panama City in February 2001. Carnaval is a four-day festival that is celebrated throughout the country just before the Christian season of Lent begins. (Right) A woman shows off her *pollera*, the traditional dress of Panama.

6 Carnaval: The All-Panama Festival

MANY TOWNS IN Panama have parades, fairs, and festivals tied to local holidays or customs. The Festival of the Black Christ at Portobelo on October 21, for example, includes a parade of the famous life-size statue of the Black Christ, and attracts pilgrims from all over the country. But the celebration that involves all of Panama is Carnaval.

Panama's Carnaval is the same as New Orleans' famed Mardi Gras. Traditionally, it's supposed to be the last chance to have fun before the 40 days of **Lent** begin. Carnaval is celebrated over the four days preceding Ash Wednesday and involves music, dancing, and a big parade on Shrove Tuesday. The celebrations in Panama City and Las Tablas are the most festive. The Semana Santa (Easter Week) celebrations at Villa de Los Santos, on the Península de Azuero, are also heavily attended.

Carnaval and the Canal Zone

Celebrated since the early 1900s, Panama's Carnaval officially begins the fourth day before Ash Wednesday, though many celebrations begin earlier. On the actual Carnaval days, most work comes to a stop and the main streets of Panama City are filled with parades, floats, masks, costumes, and confetti.

As Carnaval grew in importance in Panama, it did so in the Canal Zone as well. When the building of the Canal was almost complete, Americans joined in the four-day festivities. According to some sources, Admiral H. H. Rousseau ordered electric lights installed in the Colón Park for the Carnaval celebrations of 1912.

The following year, the Panamanian president of Carnaval asked the Americans to supply "a first-class battle-ship" on which the Carnaval Queen could make her formal entry into the city. A battleship wasn't available, so he

Did You Know?

These are the official holidays in Panama. Other occasions are celebrated with parties and carnivals or family get-togethers. In addition, many towns hold a *festejo*, or festival, to honor its patron saint.

- January 1—New Year's Day
- January 9—National Day of Mourning
- February—Carnaval
- March/April—Good Friday
- March/April—Easter
- May 1—Labor Day
- August 15—Foundation of Panama (Panama City only)
- November 2—All Soul's Day
- November 3—Independence Proclamation (from Colombia)
- November 4—The Flag's Day
- November 10—Independence Proclamation
- November 28—Independence from Spain
- December 8—Mother's Day
- December 25—Christmas Day

settled for a specially decorated tugboat instead. The Canal opened for business in 1914. In later years, one of the Panama Canal's narrow-gauge locomotives brought the Carnaval Queen to the opening ceremonies in grand style in a special parlor car.

A colorful decorated bus passes through the streets of Panama City during Carnaval.

Four Days of Fun

On Friday evening, the celebration officially begins with the selection the Carnaval Queen and her attendants. The queen then reigns over the parade and other activities. The cities best hotels sponsor dinners and dances with themes, such as "Cuban Week" at the El Panama, "Dominican Republic Week" at the Caesar Park, and "Puerto Rican Week" at the Riande Continental.

On Saturday, the main street of Panama City, Vía España, fills with people for an outdoor party. There is a small parade, music can be heard

A parading band provides a salsa beat on the streets of Panama City in February 2001 during the Panama Carnaval. Salsa is a popular Latin American dance music, which combines elements of jazz and rock with rhythmic Afro-Cuban melodies.

everywhere—mostly salsa, traditional Panamanian music, or Afro-Cuban melodies—and street vendors sell food and drinks. In the evening, the celebration moves indoors to Panama City's many discos, bars, and hotels.

A favorite Carnaval tradition is the *mojaderas*, or drenchings with water. Anyone becomes a target for fire hoses, water balloons, and buckets. On a hot tropical day, a soaking with cold water feels good.

On Sunday, at midday, there is a large, beautiful *pollera* parade. *Polleras* are Panama's national costume, and thousands of women and girls deck themselves out in the national dress to participate in the parade. Monday features another small parade, and outdoor eating and drinking continues.

Fat Tuesday is the biggest Carnaval celebration day. A huge New Orleans-style parade winds through the center of the city with highly decorated floats and costumed people from all sectors of society. Carnaval continues all day Tuesday, and winds down in the early hours of the morning on Ash Wednesday.

Recipes

Rice with Guandu

(Makes approximately eight servings)
2 cups of uncooked rice
1 cup of guandu (canned pigeon peas or black-eyed peas)
1 12-oz. can or bag of unsweetened shredded coconut
1 tablespoon of sugar
5 cups of water
salt to taste

Directions:
1. Add rice to water. Boil covered until water is nearly gone.
2. Add coconut, guandu, sugar, and salt.
3. Cook a few more minutes until the coconut is soft and guandu is hot.

Tortilla de Maiz con Queso Blanco (Corn Tortilla with Farmer's Cheese)

(Makes approximately eight servings)
2 cups masa (corn flour)
1 cup white farmer's cheese (grated)
2 eggs, beaten
1 tablespoon oil
1/4 teaspoon salt
3 tablespoons oil for frying pan

Directions:
1. Mix together all ingredients, and form into disks 1/2-inch thick and about 3 inches in diameter.
2. Fry in oil on both sides until slightly browned. Serve.

Ceviche De Garbanzos

(Makes approximately eight servings)
3 12-oz. cans of garbanzo beans or chickpeas
1/2 cup cider vinegar
1 cup olive oil
1 finely chopped onion
2 to 3 tablespoons fresh chopped parsley
2 teaspoons dried oregano leaves
3 cloves of garlic, finely minced
1 tablespoon ketchup
1 cup fresh or frozen corn
salt and cayenne pepper to taste

Directions:
1. Mix all ingredients in a large glass bowl, and cover with plastic wrap.
2. Let stand in the refrigerator overnight. Serve cold.

Chicha de Papaya (Papaya Fruit Drink)

(Makes approximately six servings)
2 cups cut up papaya (peeled and seeded)
1 cup pineapple juice
1/2 cup lime or lemon juice
1-1/2 cups papaya (or peach or apricot) nectar
1 cup ice cubes
2 cups sparkling water, ginger ale, or 7-Up

Directions:
1. Blend the first five ingredients thoroughly in blender.
2. Pour in a pitcher, and add 2 cups sparkling water, ginger ale, or 7-Up. Serve over ice and enjoy!

Pie De Limon (Lemon Pie)
(Makes approximately eight servings)
For the crust:
>2 cups thoroughly crushed vanilla wafers (2 cups after crushing)
>1 stick unsalted butter, melted

For the filling:
>1-1/2 cups sweetened condensed milk
>3/4 cup fresh lemon juice
>4 large egg yolks

Directions:
1. Preheat oven to 350° F.
2. Mix the crushed wafers with the melted butter, and press well onto a 9-inch pie dish.
3. Bake for 10 minutes, and let cool.
4. To make the filling, beat the milk with the egg yolks, and gradually add the lemon juice. This mix will curdle slightly.
5. Pour into baked cookie shell, and bake at 350° F for 10 minutes. The center of the pie should be firm to the touch.
6. Let cool completely.
7. Chill. Serve with whipped cream.

Hojaldres
(Serves four to six)
2-1/2 cups of flour
1/2 cup oil
1/2 cup milk or water
1-1/2 teaspoons baking powder
2 teaspoons salt
1 teaspoon sugar
3 cups oil

Directions:
1. Mix the 1/2 cup oil with the milk, salt, and sugar.
2. Add the baking powder to the flour, and mix dry. Then add a mixture of the milk, salt, and sugar. Stir with a fork until completely mixed.
3. Allow batch to sit for an hour.
4. Make little thick pancakes about 3 inches across.
5. Deep-fry them in 3 cups of oil (Be careful; use a slotted spoon to remove each piece.)
6. Place each one on a plate with a piece of paper to absorb any excess oil. Add butter, sugar, or powdered sugar.

Glossary

Archipelago—an expanse of water with many scattered islands in it.

Cede—to yield or grant, typically by treaty.

Civic—having to do with citizens or a city.

Civil liberties—freedom from reckless governmental control; the right of free speech, for instance.

Conquistador—Spanish for "one who conquers."

Custom duties—a tax on imports.

Dual nationality—having the legal standing of having two nationalities, American and Panamanian, for example .

Duty—a tax on imports.

Elite—a privileged group.

Fauna—the animal life of a region.

Flora—the plant life of a region.

Free trade zone—a place where no taxes or duties are paid on goods.

Froze—stopped all money transactions.

Indict—to charge with a crime by the finding or presentment of a grand jury in due form of law.

Isthmus—a narrow strip of land connecting two larger areas of land.

Junta—a group of persons who control a government, especially after a revolution or violent takeover.

Lent—the period of 40 days between Ash Wednesday and Easter Sunday, which is observed by the Roman Catholic, Eastern Orthodox, and some Protestant churches as a period of prayer and fasting.

Locks—an enclosure within a canal with gates at either end; this allows the water level in the lock to be raised and lowered. A system of locks is necessary when a canal's route must overcome a rise in elevation.

Money laundering—illegal methods of concealing money.

Nationalist—favoring a strong national government.

Peninsula—a portion of land nearly surrounded by water and connected to a larger body of land.

Plebiscite—a vote by which the people of an entire country express an opinion.

Regime—a period of rule by a particular government, especially one that is considered to be oppressive.

Revenue—the total income produced by a given source.

Tonnage—total weight in tons shipped.

Trade winds—constant winds aiding sailing ships near the equator.

Project and Report Ideas

Maps and Charts

- Show where the trade winds are found near the equator. Explain to the class how they assisted sailing ships in reaching their destinations.
- Choose either the plants or animals (fish or jungle animals) of Panama, and make a chart showing an illustration of each and a brief description of it. Or, cut out your illustrations and make mobiles to hang in class.
- Create a drawing of the Panama Canal Zone. You can find excellent maps and pictures at www.czbrats.com/cz_brats.htm, where a camera is trained on the Canal 24 hours a day.
- Draw a large map of Panama. Leave room in the margins to write one-paragraph descriptions of jungle or forest animals that live in Panama.

Flashcards

Using the glossary in this book, create flashcards. Put the term on one side and the definition on the other. Practice with the cards in pairs. Then, choose two teams of three. Select a referee to say the term out loud, and then call on someone to give the definition. The referee's decision is final. Award points for each correct answer. You can also read the definition, and ask for the correct term instead!

Cross-Curricular Reports

Write one-page, five-paragraph reports answering any of the following questions. Begin with a paragraph of introduction, then three paragraphs each developing one main idea, followed by a conclusion that summarizes your topic:

- How do canal locks work? Where are there other famous canals of this type? (You may have to use a visual aid.)
- How did malaria interfere with attempts to build the Panama Canal? How was this disease conquered and by whom?

- What happened to the gold taken from Central and South America by the Spanish? Where was it taken from?
- How can a giant ship be raised by water flowing into a canal? Explain the Archimedean Principle of displacement.
- Who were conquistadors? What was their mission?
- Find an example of one type of salsa music. Play it for the class, and explain it in your report.
- Are all rainforests the same all over the world? What characteristics do they share?

Reports

Write one-page reports on any of the following topics:
- The *Camino Real*, or Royal Road
- Vasco Núñez de Balboa's march across the Isthmus
- Ferdinand de Lesseps and the French company that attempted the first canal
- Operation Just Cause and the invasion of Panama
- General Manuel Noriega
- The harpy eagle, the national bird of Panama
- The Colón Free Zone
- Best Web sites on Panama (at least 10)

Chronology

Prehistory More than 60 Indian tribes live in Panama, connected with the Mayas of Guatemala and Mexico and the Chibchas of Colombia.

1501 Rodrigo de Bastidas, sailing westward from Venezuela, arrives in search of gold.

1502 Christopher Columbus establishes a short-lived settlement on the isthmus.

1510 The Spanish establish Santa María la Antigua del Darien, the first mainland settlement in the Americas.

1513 Vasco Núñez de Balboa marches from the Atlantic to the Pacific, proving that crossing the isthmus is the shortest route between the oceans.

1821 Panama declares independence from Spain.

1880–1900 A French company led by Ferdinand de Lesseps attempts unsuccessfully to construct a sea-level canal on the site of the present Panama Canal.

1903 Panama proclaims its independence from Columbia and concludes the Hay/Bunau-Varilla Treaty with the United States.

1914 United States completes the existing 50-mile (83 km) Panama Canal.

1964 Anti-United States riots over control of the Canal result in the deaths of four U.S. Marines and more than 20 Panamanians.

1968 The commander of the National Guard, General Omar Torrijos, establishes a military government.

1973 Secretary of State Henry Kissinger and his Panamanian counterpart, Juan Antonio Tack, craft a set of principles to guide the creation of new canal treaties.

1977	President Jimmy Carter and General Torrijos sign the Panama Canal Treaties.
1978	U.S. Senate ratifies the Panama Canal Treaty and the Neutrality Treaty, which guarantees that the canal will be open to all nations.
1981	General Torrijos' death heightens the power of the Panama Defense Force (PDF).
1984	The PDF wins most of the seats in the Legislative Assembly despite charges of corruption; at the head of the PDF is General Manuel Noriega.
1987	The United States freezes economic and military assistance to Panama because of an attack on the U.S. embassy.
1988	General Noriega is indicted in U.S. courts on drug-trafficking charges.
1989	On December 20, U.S. president George Bush orders the U.S. military into Panama; Noriega surrenders on December 27; Panama's Electoral Tribunal confirms the victory of Guillermo Endara in an earlier presidential election, the results of which had been declared invalid by Noriega.
1994	Ernesto Perez Balladares win the presidency in Panama's largest election ever.
1999	Mireya Moscoso defeats candidate Martín Torrijos, son of the late dictator; on December 31, the United States turns over control of the Panama Canal to Panama.
2002	Latin American leaders meet in Argentina for the Global Alumni Conference to discuss technological and economic issues.

Further Reading/Internet Resources

Hassig, Susan M. *Panama.* New York: Marshall Cavendish, 1996.

Haynes, Tricia. *Panama.* Philadelphia: Chelsea House, 1998.

Henderson, James D. *A Reference Guide to Latin American History.* Armonk, N.Y.: M. E. Sharpe, 2000.

Mann, Elizabeth. *The Panama Canal.* New York: Mikaya Press, 1998.

Rau, Dana Meachen. *Panama.* Danbury, Conn.: Children's Press, 1999.

Ridgely, Robert, and John Gwynn Jr. *The Guide to the Birds of Panama.* Princeton: Princeton University Press, 1992.

The Panama Canal

www.czbrats.com/cz_brats.htm

History and Geography

http://geography.about.com/library/maps/blpanama.htm?once=true&
http://www.centralamerica.com/panama/
http://lcweb2.loc.gov/frd/cs/patoc.html
http://www.alphaluz.com/panama/panami.html

Economic and Political Information

http://www.latinsynergy.org/panamainfo.htm
http://www.cia.gov/cia/publications/factbook/geos/pm.html
http://www.state.gov/www/background_notes/panama_0100_bgn.html

Culture and Festivals

http://www.worldheadquarters.com/panama/people/
http://www.alphaluz.com/panama/panamp.html
http://www.eia.doe.gov/emeu/cabs/panama.html
http://www.czbrats.com/MiNombre/carnival.htm

American Chamber of Commerce & Industry in Panama
Estafeta Balboa
Apartado 168
Panama, Republica de Panama
(507) 269-3881
(507) 223-3508
E-mail: amcham@pan.gbm.net

Republic of Panama, Embassy
2862 McGill Terrace N.W.
Washington, D.C. 20008
(202) 483-1407
Home page: http://www.embassy.pa.org

U.S. Department of Commerce International Trade Administration
Office of Latin America and the Caribbean
14th and Constitution NW
Washington, D.C. 20230
 (202) 482-0057
800-USA-TRADE
(202) 482-0464
Home page: http://www.ita.doc.gov

Index

Amerindian, 9, 16, 33, 35
Atlantic Ocean, 16, 17, 24, 26, 37

Balboa, Vasco Núñez de, 16
Balladares, Ernesto Pérez, 19
Bastidas, Rodrigo de, 15
Bush, George, 19

Canal Zone, 10, 12, 13, 20, 29, 35, 37, 48
Cape Horn, 25
Caribbean Sea, 10, 11, 13, 27, 35, 36, 43
Carnaval, 47–51
Carter, Jimmy, 21
Central America, 9, 24, 27, 29, 33, 36, 37
Colombia, 9, 17, 43
Colón, 11, 23, 26–27, 36, 41, 43, 48
Colón Free Zone, 23, 26–27, 36
Columbus, Christopher, 16
Costa Rica, 9, 10, 12

Endara, Guillermo, 19

Guzman, Antonio Tello de, 17

Hay/Bunau-Varilla Treaty, 20

Kissinger, Henry, 21

Lesseps, Ferdinand de, 17

Madrid, Arnulfo Arias, 18
Moscoso, Mireya, 20

National Guard, 18
Neutrality Treaty, 21
Noriega, Manuel, 18–19, 25
North America, 15, 34, 43

Operation Just Cause, 19

Pacific Ocean, 10, 11, 13, 16, 17, 24, 37, 44, 45
Panama
    cultures of, 33–37
    customs of, 39–45, 47–51
    economy of, 23–31, 44
    geography of, 9–13
    history of, 15–21
Panama Canal, 9, 10, 11, 12, 17, 19, 21, 23–25, 36, 41–42, 45, 48–49
Panama Canal Treaties, 21, 30
Panama City, 11, 33, 36, 37, 41–42, 43, 45, 47, 48, 50
Panama Defense Force (PDF), 18
Pearl Islands, 11, 44

Reagan, Ronald, 18
Roman Catholics, 35
Rousseau, H.H., 48
Royal Road (Camino Real), 16, 17

Santa María la Antigua del Darien, 16
South America, 9, 15, 17, 24, 27
Spanish, 9, 15, 16, 17, 24, 33, 34, 36

Tack, Juan Antonio, 21
Torrijos, Martín, 20
Torrijos, Omar, 18, 21

United States, 11, 12, 17, 18, 20, 21, 23, 26, 30–31

Venezuela, 15, 29

Picture Credits

Contributors

Senior Consulting Editor **James D. Henderson** is professor of international studies at Coastal Carolina University. He is the author of *Conservative Thought in Twentieth Century Latin America: The Ideals of Laureano Gómez* (1988; Spanish edition *Las ideas de Laureano Gómez* published in 1985); *When Colombia Bled: A History of the Violence in Tolima* (1985; Spanish edition *Cuando Colombia se desangró, una historia de la Violencia en metrópoli y provincia*, 1984); and co-author of *A Reference Guide to Latin American History* (2000) and *Ten Notable Women of Latin America* (1978).

Mr. Henderson earned a bachelors degree in history from Centenary College of Louisiana, and a masters degree in history from the University of Arizona. He then spent three years in the Peace Corps, serving in Colombia, before earning his doctorate in Latin American history in 1972 at Texas Christian University.

Charles J. Shields, the author of all eight books in the DISCOVERING CENTRAL AMERICA series, lives in Homewood, a suburb of Chicago, with his wife Guadalupe, an elementary-school principal. He has a degree in history from the University of Illinois in Urbana-Champaign, and was chairman of the English department and the guidance department at Homewood-Flossmoor High School in Flossmoor, Illinois.